elegy for [lukas]:

poems

elegy for [lukas]

luna rey hall

QUERENCIA

Querencia Press - Chicago IL

QUERENCIA PRESS

ISBN 978 1 963643 45 0

www.querenciapress.com

First Published in 2025

Querencia Press, LLC
Chicago IL

Printed & Bound in the United States of America

ALSO BY LUNA REY HALL

the patient routine

loudest when startled

no matter the diagnosis

It is a lucky thing to be alive
　　　　　　　　　　– Ada Limón

contents

[samaras]

fell asleep / under the silver / maple
body / a curled finger / awoken /

/ in the iridescent blinking of autumn /
by the papery / wings of a samara /

tumbling down / my nose / tiny helicopter
landed in my lap / dreary / i pinch it /

by the seam / bulbous ovary
between my fingers / before tossing it /

back up / into the air / & how the wind takes it /
an impulsive flutter / how it ballets

/ to the ground / like it would have
/ before i impeded / its path

trans [zombies]

it goes like this / every time /
common cold & / blood sneeze / viral

anxiety / organ plaster / a parade
of intestines / public panic / & slaughterhouse /

soldiers aiming at / civilians
/ the humvee / over-turned / bullets

unspooling brains / skulls
of mulch / a family / escapes the hysteria

/ countryside abandoned / home / another
near escape / biochemical / trepidation

/ bleach kissed / bite wound
/ mall bathroom / on sale / rib cage dress /

leaving the friend or mother or brother
/ behind / chained to the stall / everybody

saying the person / they knew
/ no longer exists

trans [extinction]

is this how it feels
/ is this considered natural causes /

or man-made / is this dehumanizing
/ is this second place / to a harry potter game

/ & die-ins & / mustache drawn / chin etched in stone
/ is this *tranny faggot in your way*

/ is this our punishment
for existing

/ for having a spot / in history /
millions upon / millions / have gone extinct /

that we / don't even know about
/ before / they had a chance / before

they were given names / before they were
/ /

wearing [dresses] for the first time

"do you want me to be honest" / my mother says / after this long pause over the phone
/ i had just told her how uncomfortable / i felt at work all day /

the luminous fixations / the / let / me / turn / my / head / away / from / your
/ non-binary / -ass / looks / the chewing at the surface / of my lips /

until they were raw / an anxious tic / all day / turned wild shame
/ dancing / throbbing shame / molten booms of lightning shame

yeah / i finally reply / the word tumbling off the cliff / of my swollen lip /
"i'm just absorbing / what you told me / first the new pronouns

/ now the women's clothing / does it mean you were a woman today
or how does that work" / i can hear the quivering swell /

in her breathing / the strained coughing / between sobs /
"i'm sorry / that i don't / quite / understand" /

i feel bad for [the body]

all the razor burn / muscle fatigue
/ benign mole & skin tags /

all the urinal nightmares
/ & limp ache / the violence

/ exit wounds / all the protein /
ablation / tender-free /

& solitude skin / the days after days
of / aluminum / scabs /

bronchial exhaust / & assertive
pattern recession

/ i feel bad for [the body] /
when i say who

/ has ever wanted you
/ [the body] that got me this far /

[sisterhood]

my sister worries / she made me trans
/ by tugging a dress over my head

/ when i was little / like Vesuvius in lace /
the stars shattered

/ violet dust / all of heaven
shrouded over me

/ fuchsia glitter / & sparks /
the gasp & awe

/ brushed-on eyebrows / a flicker /
of foundation

/ try olive / try honey / try almond & bisque
/ then show & tell /

for the whole family / but
/ i don't remember

any of that / only the story /
i wish i did /

i wish i had that moment / dancing /
on my brain stem /

a / single / moment / a single joyous moment
/ as her sister

[gender reveal parties]

computer screen backlight / chrome
tab / arrow / hovering over / a planned parenthood video /

how to perform an intramuscular (IM) self-Injection
/ on mute / closed-captions to follow along with /

what am i doing / spending my friday night
body layered in sweater / sweater / sweater /

what am i doing / spending my life / this way /
i'm alone in my room / a party popper in hand /

pop /
confetti burying me / in its colors

trans [silence]

everything [the boy] says is true / all the harm i put him through /
i've seen enough films to know who the real villain is

/ rope tight skin / mini-van a cage / nightsky skin /
& when / he finally escapes / & he's almost / free /

& the daylight is seeping / through everything & / someone
is there / to save him / & i'm right behind

putting on my best show / a knife to his back / ominous music kicks in /
& i whisper in his ear / the subtitles say

/ if you say another word / then you're dead / & he just had to
/ he just had to say something / to save me

every line is an attempt at [the body]

jupiter ash & star matter
/ starved / bone bleach /

a realm / a massacre
/ overwhelming riot /

yellow-pink snapdragon
/ thumb rubbing the throat

/ mouth squeezed open / shouting /
shame

/ shaved down to blood & burn
/ grapeseed oil skin / puppet

/ a ghost story
/ a cocoon /

bra strap / shoulder bite
/ cross arm pullover top

/ tiny pockets / full of little deaths
/ under-tongue pill & / bloodstream

/ purple matte / lustrous cigarette
/ "are / you / pregnant or

/ might / become pregnant?" /
parasite & host

/ welcoming the cat call
/ face pressed against the pillow

/ bills that forget the dead name
/ scrunchie wrist / duchess slant /

"hello miss" / eyebrow arch /
mary jane pumps / all of heaven

/ a kingdom of forgiveness /
a shadow / in the shape of hips

in love with [the body]

eventide / thick / birch tree / autumn air / cold
/ enough / to make her nipples / hard / cold

buttons against / a thin blouse / but that made her
feel cute / that made her feel / her /

/ & there is love / the whole of [the body]
/ & there is love

[nail polish] prayer

lacquer me holy father / paint me stars & glitter /   *we don't pray like that*
pardon the sinful brush / spill over /   *we don't pray like that*

goodness & faithful /   *we don't pray like that*
unmerited neon – abounding grace /   *we don't pray like that*

i know that if i do this /   *we don't pray like that*
ultra violet eyes watch over me /

my waking hours / gel cured omnipotence /
measure my divergence /   *we don't pray like that*

eggshell clear / manicure /
walk with my decisions / opalescent guidance /   *we don't pray like that*

& acetone /   *we don't pray like that*
& chaste & pure /

the half-moon resin / lunula neglect /   *we don't pray like that*
forgive me /   */ amen /*

let me be me /   *we don't pray like that*
let me ~~be me~~   *~~we don't~~ pray like that*

23

[motherhood]

there is a universe where i am a mother /
chiffon mouth / sugar lips /

bread-baked stomach /
hips swallowed by the shallowest of tides /

there is a universe where i am a mother /
a barren womb / dormant inside /

sand-blasted / oven scraped
/ receding tide /

there is a universe where i am a mother
/ please, nestle the tide /

a bassinet of grief /
there is a universe where i am a mother /

[the boy]'s locker room / superstar
/ mommy's golden dime / basketball god /

all natural / protein shake / cheering
boy / it's okay to dance /

rigid upwelling / spring blooms /
there is a universe where i am a mother /

children delivered / tumor farm /
eddy my lungs / misunderstood cells /

cells children / children
athirst / athirst for the chemical bath /

there is a universe where i am a mother /
/   /   /

/
/

there is a universe where i am a mother /
riesling iris & wrinkles & beach date & /

lake ebbing the beach & sand-stuck sunglasses
/ & grandchildren & grandchildren & grandchildren /

&
/

there is a universe where i am a mother /
all that was robbed from me /

what should have been / how the moon gifts tides
/ & asks nothing in return /

[being a woman]

i keep writing the same joke / a body walks into a bar
/ & i don't recognize it /

the problem is
/ i don't think there's a punchline to the joke /

the punchline was creation / white trident / eggshell
/ spoiled bed sheets / the punchline was birth

/ naked whine / we got another one
/ [the boy] chorus / [the body] made entirely of salt

/ broken bones / rawhide future /
the punchline was shaking / like it knew

/ puzzling mess / confusion & pulp & indecision
& grief / & that / too / is my crime

/ & growth / internal wobbling / the soft palate
/ genital hysteria / dress-up & spit shine & visiting the morgue

/ maybe / the punchline is /
a body walks into a bar / & / i'm starting to recognize it

[clay]

another body i couldn't inhabit
/ the grief of another husk

/ *i am a failure* /

the clay / glazed earthen hands
/ pinched hips / slab stomach

/ thrown triceps & scored beard
/ kneaded eyes / bottom thinned

/ *i am a failure* /

all the slip that never hardened
/ wet mudslide off my palms

/ [the body] deserved a kiln / a fire
/ to perfect it

[flowers]

in the cool soil / he planted snapdragons /
the most boyish flower he could dream of /

amber & salmon & mauve snouts lapping
the stream / from the watering kettle

/ & when approached by his brother /
saying "are you playing with flowers again / ?"

he'd say no / no / it's not a flower
/ it's a dragon /

his tiny fingers / squeezing / the petals shut
& making a noise / like fire

[fatherhood]

hose reel nest / no mother in sight
/ he scoops the twig home /

baby sparrow song / his palms
leaf & rotten bark / spider film /

he showed his father
the bird / look i'm a mama

bird / taking care of it
with a worm / pinky wiggling

by its beak / & he was scolded /
"you can't be a mama bird" /

"mothers abandon
the child if a human /

touches them" / & he had
/ his thumb feather soft /

from petting / now /
"you'll have to take care of it

in another way" / his father
vanished in the spring mist

/ & he sat there / under the deck /
watching the sparrow twitter

around the pavement / tiny feet
chittering in the acoustics

/ when his father returned with
the biggest rock he could find

/ & handed it to him

[dancing]

alone / in his room /
feet bobbing off the bed

/ off-rhythm / a quiet hum
of blood / kick drum heart /

lying back / forearms / & /
hands tucked underneath

him / popcorn ceiling dancing
to the song in his head /

[the boy] shut tight /
his eyes & imagined /

hardwood ballroom /
sprung floor / everybody

watching him become / chiffon /
lace / & / spandex /

the skirt whisking
/ into a moon /

gay [piercings]

[the boy] learns about the gay ear / again /
the piercing / the one with all the glittered wax /

a sore of shame / he's been warned / he shouldn't have a gay ear
/ a gay nostril / or gay lip or eyebrow or septum or /

he didn't want to end up / like his uncle with the gay nipple /
he didn't want to end up / [the] ~~gay~~ [boy] /

the only thing in his mind / on par / with mormon crickets
/ a real plague / on par with an apple & woman

/ a real plague / or / [the boy] just wanted /
one small turquoise jewel / just one dot

/ in an ocean of skin / one thing he could look at /
in the mirror / & see part of himself /

playing with [dolls]

there in an   /   empty field   /   thistle between   /   the teeth
/   [the boy] plays   /   with a doll   /   he stole from the house   /

his mother cleans   /   once a week   /   palms full   /   of dogwood   /
& bluestem   /   all he pushed aside   /   the smeared   /   plant residue

/   clothing the   /   naked doll   /   before it starts   /   to rain   /
condensation on   /   plastic skin   /   on confused skin   /   [the boy]

/   looks up to the sky   /   eyes flinching   /   with each   /
droplet   /   that   /   makes   /   contact

[retirement]

he wanted to retire / simple / sign that motherfucker up / for social security
/ put him in old man home / pension his tongue / real piggy-bank fat /

let him get bored / become a store greeter / babysit his grandchildren
/ let him have grandchildren / get him a few hobbies / a few more /

write that novel he always talked about / gym talker instead of lifter
/ learn french & / the words / compound / asset / cash flow / diverse

/ stratosphere wealth / buy a summer home / seasonal change
/ join a facebook group just once / radicalize him / let him yell

at the sky / paint his fist red / white / & blue / he had a whole plan
/ a notebook / a checklist / ten easy steps for a happier retirement /

you could say [the boy] did it / you could say he did retire /
it just came a whole lot earlier / than either of us / ever thought it would

[fabric]

we find [the boy] in the textile aisle
/ memorized

by this orange-green / ugly duckling
/ roll of fabric /

his tiny hands consumed
/ by something he never felt before /

blanket material / the knitted fuzz
/ billowy bounce / cotton brushed /

his mind a void
/ a delicate / delicate void

/ he hadn't considered / how soft
/ the world could be

we are all [stardust]

he was made from the star /
dust smashed together

/ a cosmic orchid /
abloom / petals aflame /

presolar / extracted light /
volatile compass / & heart

/ the whole nebula of a person /

when one blinks out
/ another takes its place

/ there are billions of stars in the sky
/ & i'll always know / where he was

[the boy]

i perform it lovely /
the death of [the boy] /

i pick the location
/ to be buried

/ the yellow birch tomb /
underground

root mouth / schedule
the candlelight

vigils / around /
father's work schedule

/ & mother's cancer
appointments

/ the midnight zone /
church service /

the condolence / monsoon
/ "you're a poet"

/ so they ask me /
to write the obit /

to make it iron
/ make it loud /

make it a deep
/ red grief

/ throbbing
in the arterial / home

/ & i perform it
/ lovely /

the headstone / liquor /
awkward / family silence

/ the bible /
thump /

& mournful mist
/ & casket soiled

brown / the summer
/ salt tear down

my cheek /
all to fall asleep

/ on my parent's couch
/ & wake up

/ the next day /
& next day /

& the next / &
/ & / &

acknowledgments

thank you to the editors of the following journals for publishing early versions of poems, sometimes under different names, contained in this book:

"[dancing]" (the boy wanted to dance) – *HAD*

"trans [extinction]" (trans extinction) – *HAD*

"[gender reveal parties]" (gender reveal party) – *paper teeth press*

"[fatherhood]" (the boy wanted a baby) – *paper teeth press*

"trans [zombies]" (trans zombie film) – *A Dozen Nothing*

"[samaras]" (samara fruit) – *A Dozen Nothing*

"wearing [dresses] for the first time" (wearing a dress for the first time) – *Water~Stone Review*

"i feel bad for [the body]" – Rock Paper Poem

Querencia Press, especially Emily Perkovich: thank you for giving these poems a home. Jihyun Yun, Matthew Dickman, Kayleb Rae Candrilli, and Claire Wahmanholm: thank you for your kind words. all my friends, family, fellow poets, and trans siblings: thank you for your encouragement, friendship, love, and time. reader: thank you.

www.ingramcontent.com/pod-product-compliance
Lightning Source LLC
Chambersburg PA
CBHW081726120626
46550CB00010B/3265